New Moon

Writing

How to Express Yourself with Passion and Practice

The New Moon Books Girls Editorial Board

Flynn Berry · Lauren Calhoun · Ashley Cofell

Morgan Fykes · Katie Hedberg · Elizabeth Larsson

Priscilla Mendoza · Julia Peters-Axtell · Caitlin Stern

CROWN PUBLISHERS, INC. ⋆ NEW YORK

For every girl who has been moved to put
her dreams in writing

Text copyright © 2000 by New Moon Publishing, Inc.

Published by Crown Publishers, a division of Random House, Inc.,
201 East 50th Street, New York, New York 10022.

CROWN and colophon are trademarks of Random House, Inc.

www.randomhouse.com/kids

Library of Congress Cataloging-in-Publication Data
New Moon Books Girls Editorial Board.
New moon. Writing / the New moon books girls editorial board.
p.   cm.
Summary: Explores the various outlets for expressing yourself through writing, including plays, poetry, and personal essays. Includes suggestions for improving writing and places to get published.
ISBN 0-517-88587-5 (trade pbk.) — ISBN 0-517-88588-3 (lib. bdg.)
1. Children as authors — Handbooks, manuals, etc. — Juvenile literature. 2. Girls — Authorship — Marketing — Handbooks, manuals, etc. — Juvenile literature. 3. Journalism — Authorship — Handbooks, manuals, etc. — Juvenile literature. 4. Creative writing — Handbooks, manuals, etc. — Juvenile literature. [1. Creative writing. 2. Authorship.] I. Title.
PN171.C5 N49   2000
808'.02'08352 — dc21   99-048906

Printed in the United States of America
February 2000

10 9 8 7 6 5 4 3 2 1
First Edition

New Moon is a registered trademark of New Moon Publishing, Inc.

CONTENTS

The folks who made this book want to thank all the people who gave such enthusiastic help and who believe so strongly in Listening to Girls!

The Girls Editorial Board of *New Moon: The Magazine for Girls and Their Dreams,* the girls who read and create *New Moon Magazine,* the New Moon Publishing team, and our parents.

Jennifer Cecil, Sheila Eldred, Seth Godin Productions, Bridget Grosser, Mavis Gruver, Debra Kass Orenstein, Joe Kelly, Nia Kelly, Erin Lyons, Jason Mandell, Deb Mylin, Sarah Silbert, Barbara Stretchberry, and Ann Weinerman.

Our colleagues at Lark Productions: Robin Dellabough, Lisa DiMona, and Karen Watts.

And our friends at Crown Publishing: Simon Boughton, Andrea Cascardi, Michelle Gengaro-Kokmen, Nancy Hinkel, and Isabel Warren-Lynch.

NOTE FROM *NEW MOON'S* FOUNDER

New Moon is a magazine that gives girls the power to believe in ourselves, to help us stand up for what we think is right, and, most of all, to let us just be girls. *New Moon* sends a message that makes a girl feel, "However I am, I'm okay." *New Moon* describes girls who take action when things are unfair, instead of keeping quiet. And *New Moon* is a fun, safe place where girls know that they are not alone.

New Moon: The Magazine for Girls and Their Dreams is an international, advertising-free bimonthly that is edited BY girls between ages 8 and 14. The recipient of dozens of awards, *New Moon* was twice named winner of the Parents' Choice Foundation Gold Award — the only child-edited magazine ever to win that honor. Begun in 1993, *New Moon* is a girl-driven alternative to magazines and other media that focus on how girls look. *New Moon*'s slant is that makeup, boys, and fashion are important to girls, but they represent maybe three degrees of a girl's life. *New Moon* focuses on the other 357 degrees of a thinking girl's life. Instead of telling girls who they *should* be, *New Moon* tells the world who girls really *are*.

This series of New Moon Books continues that mission. Our books talk about real issues and real girls. They don't say, "This is how you have to be." Instead, they share girls' experiences, feelings, and ideas. Just like *New Moon* magazine, New Moon Books are created BY girls. We chose nine *New Moon* readers from all over the country, including Alaska and Hawaii, Minnesota and New York, to work on the books. They range in age from 10 to 14 and represent home school, public school, and private school. White, Black, Filipino, and Asian, these girls have done a marvelous job, as we knew they would.

In this book, they write about writing and all its wonders. Working with Robin Dellabough of Lark Productions and Joe Kelly of New Moon Publishing, they explore different forms of the written word, from poetry to plays, letters to articles. They've profiled female writers, both famous and brand-new, and they have dozens of suggestions for ways to improve your writing, overcome writer's block, get published, and have a lot of fun with words.

We think you'll love this book because it's about how real girls are inspired to read and write. So get ready to find out more about reading and writing by Listening to Girls, which is our favorite thing to do!

Molly McKinnon
Editor, *New Moon: The Magazine for Girls and Their Dreams*

Nancy Gruver
Founder & Publisher, New Moon Publishing

 NOTE FROM THE NEW MOON BOOKS GIRLS EDITORIAL BOARD

We are very proud to be the Girls Editorial Board for these books. We hope that they will help other girls feel good about themselves and their abilities. Like you, we are strong, spirited girls. We got together at a hotel in New York to start creating the books. We had an awesome weekend, where we worked hard and played hard. We came up with ideas for most of the material in the books and had a say in everything that went into them. We chose topics that we wanted to write about, too. After that, we worked on the books and with each other over the Internet. And when each book was almost finished, we edited it and said what should change. All in all, it was a pretty amazing experience!

We appreciate New Moon's approach and feel lucky to be reaching more girls through this series of books. Sure, some of us may like boys and putting on makeup, but we also enjoy playing sports, spending time with our friends, learning about international happenings, reading, writing, and all of the other exciting things the world has to offer. That's why we researched and wrote about friendship, earning money, reading, writing, and sports — things that are important to girls in their lives. We found, in the United States and around the world, girls with competence and self-respect. We hope that you will find, in their experiences, the inspiration that every girl needs. Girls are so much more than clothes and diets; we are individuals with views and ideas, energy and talent. New Moon is our voice. Add yours and let us be heard!

Flynn Berry, age 11, New York

Lauren Calhoun, age 13, Hawaii

Ashley Cofell, age 10, Minnesota

Morgan Fykes, age 12, Washington, D.C.

Katie Hedberg, age 11, Minnesota

Elizabeth Larsson, age 12, New Jersey

Priscilla Mendoza, age 11, California

Julia Peters-Axtell, age 14, Minnesota

Caitlin Stern, age 13, Alaska

A Writing Life

CHAPTER ONE

Why Write?

Have you ever had a thought or a feeling or witnessed something that made you feel like you suddenly knew something very important? Was it an insight that made you say to yourself, "Now I understand" or, "So that's the way things work"? Maybe you were just *moved* by something and didn't know what to make of what you saw or felt. You wanted to tell someone when it happened so they could understand this amazing or beautiful or painful thing, too, or help you to understand it better. But no one was around to listen, or you didn't think you could explain it, or you didn't want to tell a person because it was too private. You had to get it out all the same because it was making you itch. And maybe the only way to scratch the itch was to write.

Writers work all their lives to learn *how* to describe what they experience so that whatever they have to say can be understood by a reader. They also write for themselves, no matter what others may think of their work. In other words, you don't have to be published to consider yourself a writer. You don't even have to *want* to be published. Plenty of wonderful writing is done in journals, as letters, and for the joy of writing itself. You can start anytime, no matter how little you've written up until now.

That's what this book is for: to encourage you to write what you feel, what you know, what you think, what you dream. It's also to let you in on some kinds of writing you might not have tried before. Ever consider writing a play? How about a poem, an essay, a travelogue, a letter to the editor, a novella, a monologue, a short story, a book review, a newspaper article, or even a song? There are as many ways to express yourself in words as there are subjects to explore through writing.

We know *you* have something to say, so go ahead and write right!

Find Your First Words' Worth

You want to write. You *need* to write. But you're clueless about how or where to begin. You're suffering from Blank Page Syndrome. What you need is inspiration to get you started! There are many ways to get your creative juices flowing. Here are a few suggestions:

- *Use your environment.* Your senses are five of your greatest tools for finding inspiration. Look around: maybe you're outdoors and the sky happens to be a shade of blue you've never seen before, or you're in your room and you notice the quilt your mother made for you. When you listen, can you hear someone else's conversation? Does their tone of voice or what they're talking about tell you something about them or about the way people communicate in general? Take in a deep breath...is that the oven cleaner you smell? Maybe it's the perfect detail for your next science fiction story.

- *Keep a dream journal.* Have you ever had a really weird, lifelike dream? We hope you wrote it down, because your own dreams can be the most creative things in the world. Keep a notebook next to your bed, and as soon as you wake up, before you get out of bed or think about what you have to do that day, stop and remember your dream as best you can. Then write down what you recall. Oftentimes, the symbols or people in your dreams are the things in your subconscious that may be affecting you the most. Taking a hint from your dreams might help you to uncover some powerful feelings in your writing.

- *Read, read, read, read!* Reading expands you and opens your mind to new things; almost everything you read affects you in one way or another, whether it's positive or negative. Maybe you read a really sexist book or article and you were so enraged that you had to write things right again. Though you didn't realize it, that book or article provided some inspiration for you. Read things similar to what you're trying to write. Try to imitate your favorite poet's style or form. Take one sentence from a story you love and write a whole different story of your own. What you're trying to do is stimulate your brain, and one of the best ways to do that is by reading what came from someone else's brain.

- *Go to a museum.* Art can be a great source of inspiration, not just a product of it. Art is like writing because it uses imagination and passion and can sometimes tell a story. Try to put into words what the artist put in the artwork. What was Mona Lisa's life like, after all? You could make up her life story, based on the painting. You might even want to take notes as you view different works. The piece of art can be a jumping-off point for you, a spark for a string of ideas, or you could choose to focus entirely on the work itself—many poems spring from a meditation on a work of art. If there isn't a museum near you, go to the library, look through art books, and read about the artists who created the paintings or sculptures you admire.

- *People-watch.* People do the strangest things sometimes, don't they? You can learn a lot about people just by watching them lead their daily lives, and what you see can make great material for short stories or poems. Pick a good spot, like a park or a shopping mall, and plant yourself inconspicuously for a while. To get a really good perspective on things, pretend you are an alien studying Earthlings and you have to explain Earth to the folks at home. Listen to the way passersby talk, and use their speech patterns when you write dialogue. Make up stories about the characters you see — the old man who walks his dog every day or the young couple with their baby. Try to imagine who these people are and why they are in that situation at that very moment. Then start writing!

- *Use your past.* Sometimes your own life is the most powerful source of inspiration. Think of how many memoirs and autobiographies there are — how many books are based on an author's personal history. To open your own memory banks, try looking through a family album, re-reading old notes from your friends, or sifting through memorabilia from camp or any other important event in your life. Try to focus on the emotions that arise in you as you relive these memories. See if you can conjure up exactly how you felt on your first day of school or what the Grand Canyon looked like at sunset on your family vacation.

HIGH PROFILE: KAREN CUSHMAN

Author Karen Cushman didn't start out as a professional writer. She had been telling stories until her husband suggested she write them down. Once she did, she was so successful, she hasn't stopped. She has written *The Mid-Wife's Apprentice*, a Newbery Medal winner; *Catherine, Called Birdy*, a Newbery Honor Book; and *The Ballad of Lucy Whipple*. Her books are based on historical research and include characters from ordinary life in the past.

New Moon: When did you decide you wanted to be a writer?

Karen Cushman: I wrote a lot when I was a child. In elementary school, I started enjoying it, but at that time I didn't know that writing could be a successful career. It was when my daughter was in college that I got the idea for *Catherine, Called Birdy*. I never knew that someday I'd be a writer.

NM: Why did you choose writing as one of the things you wanted to do?

KC: I had things to say, questions to explore, and stories to tell. I basically wanted my voice to be heard.

NM: What do you think is the best way to learn to write a story?

KC: Writing a lot! It's like exercising for a sport—the more you do it, the better you are. Also reading, getting a sense of how other people tell a story.

NM: How do you choose which stories to write?

KC: I have a lot of ideas bouncing around in my head, screaming, yelling, and hollering. The one idea that catches my attention most or yells the loudest is the one I work further on.

NM: What were some of the most difficult obstacles you had to overcome?

KC: Probably the most difficult obstacle for me to overcome would be the little self-confidence which I had. I kept hearing myself say that I was too old to write, that I couldn't do this, no one would want to read what I had to say.

NM: What advice would you give to girls about working toward their dreams?

KC: Dreams are like road maps showing you where to go. Pay attention to your dreams; go for it! It's important to have dreams.

NM: Why is writing so great?

KC: One: the matter of writing as a way to be heard. Two: the sense of accomplishment, similar to the feeling you have after finishing a difficult puzzle. Three: it's something you can care about, and something you can convince other people to care about.

NM: What can writing do for girls?

KC: Writing gives girls a voice, a sense of power.

—Priscilla, age 11, California

Writing to Discover Yourself

Surely there have been times in your life when you felt confused about a situation, or were so mad that you had truly violent thoughts, or felt so alone that you didn't know what to do with yourself. A good way of releasing all this emotional tension is to write out your feelings, even if no one ever sees what you write. It is important to vent your frustrations and anxieties, and when no one is around to listen, you can do that by writing. When you're angry at a friend, write a letter (but don't give it to her!). You might find that aside from the relief of venting, putting your thoughts down on paper will help you to say what you're feeling when you do talk to her.

Ask a Girl

"I found my little sister snooping through my room. I think she may have been looking for my journal or, worse, already found it. What should I say to her? How can I make sure that she never invades my privacy again? I don't want to write in it anymore because I am scared someone will read it."

I write EVERYTHING in my journal, and I can't even imagine what I would do if someone read it (have you read Harriet the Spy?). About your sister: you have to talk to her about this. Tell her exactly how you feel about her invading your privacy, and ask her how she would feel if you read HER journal. Involve your parents if necessary, and explain to them how important it is to you that your privacy be respected. If you still don't feel safe, get a journal with a lock or find a really good hiding place. ◊

POINT OF VIEW: *Write It Out*

Sometimes when you're mad, you say things you regret later. That's why it's better to write your thoughts on a piece of paper. Instead of blowing up, write your feelings down. You'll be amazed at how your feelings will burst out. Sometimes I write pages and pages when I'm mad. It's good to be mad and to express your anger, so let it flow out of your heart and onto the page in front of you. When I write, it takes a lot of the GRRRR out of me, and I feel peace once I'm done. I often like to rip the paper up and throw it away, or crumple it up and play soccer or some kind of contact sport with it! Try this next time you're mad. You could even get a journal for your feelings.

When my grandma died, it was very hard for me and my family. My pencil and paper were very good at consoling me. I wrote a lot of poems about her, and even a short story. I felt like all the sad emotions had been stored up in me, and the paper allowed the emotions to burst out from somewhere deep within me. At first, I couldn't write anything about my grandma, but when I went to stay in her house right before her funeral, all the memories of good times I had with her came back. The smell of her bedsheets; her dog, Toby; her jellybean jar; and all the little things you don't notice until they are gone brought her right back to me. I am still writing about her a year later. I expect the loss will never get out of my system, but I will have learned to live with the loss, and documenting it has helped.

—Lauren, age 13, Hawaii

One girl was able to turn writing about her emotions into a whole book. When she was 12, Latoya Hunter wrote a diary of her first year in a New York City junior high school. *The Diary of Latoya Hunter* was later published and became a bestseller. Latoya writes about falling in love for the first time, the murder of a local shopkeeper, arguing with her parents, school cliques, and visiting her birthplace in Jamaica. "I didn't know I had so many feelings and opinions before this," Latoya says, "because I never really had to sit down and write what I felt. I learned about myself—like that a lot of things around me affect me a lot."

Besides helping people discover how they feel, writing can help them discover more about their backgrounds: where they come from geographically, culturally, and maybe even spiritually.

How to Be the Best Writer You Can Be

CHAPTER TWO

In this chapter, we'll look at the actual physical act of writing, from the moment you pick up your pen to your tenth draft. What kind of paper do you like? What color ink? Where do you like to write? What do you do when you have writer's block? How do you know when you're finished with a piece of writing? The answers to these questions are different for every girl. That's what makes reading about famous writers so fascinating: descriptions of their unique techniques, rhythms, habits, and tricks prove that there is no one perfect process for writing. What works for someone else may not work at all for you. That said, read our suggestions, then try what appeals to you.

The Writer's Toolkit

In order to start writing, here's a checklist of things you'll need:

- *A place.* This might seem obvious, but *where* you write affects your writing. Some people find it impossible to write without total silence; others find it impossible to write without some background noise, like music or talking. What matters most is the amount of distraction you think you can handle. If you're the kind of person who works in an almost trancelike state, it would be good to find a room of your own. Your environment can also provide inspiration: snatches of other people's conversation for your fictional dialogue, the sound of waves for the rhythm of your poem, or a nearby painting for a scene description.

Your writing place needs to be comfortable, but not so comfortable you'll drift into dreamland whenever you're there. One girl might find lying on a carpeted floor her best position, while another loves nothing better than sitting at her smooth wooden desk. Experiment with different places and don't be afraid to try a spot that seems unconventional. It might inspire your best writing.

- *Pens.* Even if you plan to work mostly on a computer, you can't go without the real thing for very long. You can't take a computer with you everywhere (even if you have a laptop), and there's something satisfying about writing a poem or a passage by hand that just gets lost when you use a computer all the time. Use a good pen to put yourself in the writing mood — you'll find yourself trying to live up to the pen by writing beautifully with it! Fountain pens are the

17

nicest — and the most expensive. Rollerballs and fine-point felt-tip pens are the next best, with those dime-a-dozen ballpoint pens finishing last — though there's something to be said for disposable pens. Once you find a type or brand of pen you like, you'll never stray — writers are very loyal to their pens!

- *Paper and notebooks.* Even if you're not that into journal writing, it helps to keep a blank book at your side at all times. You never know when inspiration is going to hit, and it's nice when you have some way of grabbing your ideas and keeping them all in one place — even though some of the most famous poems began on the backs of napkins!

- *A word processor.* Sooner or later, you'll want to let someone read your work and you'll realize that the chicken scratch in your journal just won't cut it. Nothing looks better than a cleanly typed manuscript of your own work. Also, it's essential for submitting to publications. For these reasons, not to mention the obvious benefit of ease of editing, try to use a word processor if you're serious about writing. Any program will do. Some are fancier than others, but all you really need is a place to save your work and maybe a spell-checker.

Make a separate computer file for each piece of your writing and be sure to save every version of your work — you never know when you'll need that stuff you edited out of your earlier drafts. Some writers also keep "scrap files," files with bits and pieces of ideas they had or nice passages that they couldn't fit into their final versions. And *always* back up your files. Copy all of your files onto a floppy disk or the hard drive of another computer. Computers are never crash-proof, and you'll want to avoid losing any part of your work because of technical difficulties.

- *A great dictionary.* All dictionaries are not created equal. A poor one can be frustrating to use, while a good general dictionary is one you'll use on a daily basis. But we wouldn't stop there. There is a profusion (look it up!) of specialized dictionaries that can be a huge help to all kinds of writers. Check out dictionaries of synonyms, slang, clichés, and frequently misspelled words; thesauri (what's another word for thesaurus?); and the queen of them all, the grand old *Oxford English Dictionary.* (See Chapter Five for specific suggestions on the best dictionaries and other reference books.)

Ready, Set, Write!

Before you write anything — a story, an essay, or a poem — you might have a sudden flash of inspiration. Or you might not. Then you need to have a brainstorming session: a method of *creating* inspiration, finding new ideas, spurring yourself on.

Here are some of our favorite brainstorming tricks:

- *Jottings.* Jot down all your ideas at once. It is important to write down anything that crosses your mind, even if you think you may not use it, even if you think it sounds dumb or crazy.

- *The five W questions.* As you start a new work, ask yourself *Who? What? When? Where? Why?* And don't forget *How?*

- *Imagine.* List all the images that come to your mind about your subject and any specific words that you want to use.

- *Bubbles.* Pick a topic, write it in the center of a page, and circle it. Then branch out from that circle, or bubble, with more circles of things that relate to your topic and draw bubbles out from those things as well. Soon you'll have a whole web of ideas, images, and material to work from.

- *Browse.* Remember all those cool books on words and writing we mentioned? Now's the time to start putting them to good use. Sometimes your eye falls on a certain word you've never heard of and that alone sparks a whole sentence, metaphor, or plot.

Freewriting

This is a special brainstorming technique that many professional writers use to get their brains working. It's like warming up your car before you drive or warming up your muscles before you run. You pick a topic and then *write* furiously without stopping — not even to cross out, or correct your spelling — for a pre-set length of time or number of pages. The rule is you can't stop writing once you start, even if you have to write what you just wrote over again until you think of something new. It will be hard at first because you've been trained to worry about grammar and sentence structure, but when you forget about all that stuff, this exercise can be really freeing. You might be surprised by what shows up when you re-read it!

Sometimes it's fun to freewrite about a color, like what "red" makes you think of, or to use one word, like "lemonade," and just let your brain go. Maybe you'll be reminded of how your grandmother made the best lemonade and how you used to sit on her front porch and sip it at twilight when the crickets were out and how she once told you a story about why crickets sing, and then you'll realize you want to retell this story and you'll already have all this great stuff to start from. See? This technique is especially helpful when you can't think of something to write about or when you're nervous about starting a new story.

The *state of mind* that you're in when you start writing is bound to shape your material. Think about what mood is most appropriate for what you want to convey. You can make the choice. Some people find that writing in the midst of strong emotion produces the best work — like when you're feeling passionate about a movie you just saw, sit down at your desk and scribble furiously until your pencil breaks or type until you run out of paper. It might be a little hard to read when you're through *("ytou mmake ,me so made somtiems #!!.")*, but the raw emotion can be powerful and vivid. Other people feel that the best writing comes from a mind cleared of daily circumstances, so that you are free to contemplate your subject deeply and objectively. If this is true for you, find a quiet spot and let your ideas and feelings flow from there.

First Draft

So now that you have your mind ready, your pen and paper or computer in front of you, and your pages of amazing ideas on your desk you're all ready to go. Suddenly, you freeze up—you don't know what to do! You're thinking, "I can't write this, I don't even know how to begin, I'm no good. Who was I kidding? Aw, forget it, I'll do this later." Stop! Everyone goes through this; beginning is the biggest obstacle you have to overcome. You're worried that your writing is not going to turn out how you wanted it to, or that it won't be perfect. Why are you putting all this pressure on yourself? Very, very few writers write perfect first drafts. If you can't think of a beginning, start in the middle—you can always come back to the beginning. Don't procrastinate or get intimidated. Your first draft can stink worse than last week's laundry, but no one's going to see it (or smell it), so who cares?

Overcoming Writer's Block

Writing can be very frustrating. Sometimes the words just won't come out right, or your brain seems frozen. When people complain of writer's block, it means that they are stuck, not able to find the words to say what they want to express, not able to…umm, you know…kind of like now…

Try taking a break (not too long, you procrastinator, you!) or working on something else you've written. Reading someone else's short story or poem also helps to get the wheels turning. But one of the best things that you can do is go back to freewriting. Just write, "I don't have writer's block, I don't have writer's block," over and over until you think of something. Or concentrate on the word "block" and see what associations arise from that.

Sometimes you can write *about* your writer's block. If you can't beat it, join it! Sometimes you just have to get that first sentence down. Write whatever comes to mind. Eventually, you'll be on your way again. You also can talk through your writer's block. Talk with someone about the subject you want to write about. That could get your juices flowing again.

A Poem; Can't (or Maybe)

Can't think,
Can't write,
Can't get my words to flow.

Oh how I want to,
but I can't.
Or can I?

I'm Thinking I can't Think,
I'm Writing I can't Write,
My words are flowing into I can't make my words flow,

I CAN.

—Morgan, age 12, Washington, D.C.

The Next Step: Feedback

From asking someone for constructive feedback to reading
a poem out loud, there are lots of ways to share your work
with the world—when you're ready.

You might start by realizing that not everything you

write will be perfect. A helpful way to improve your writing is to ask a friend, relative, or teacher to give you some constructive criticism. She can point out where your areas of weakness are, or where you have strengths. She may notice minor spelling or grammatical errors that you overlooked. Having somebody proofread your work and offer constructive criticism will always help you improve as a writer. After all, it is *constructive* criticism.

Separating the Girl from the Writer: Revision

Any writer worth her salt will tell you the single most important part of the writing process is revising your first draft. And then maybe a second, third, fourth, and beyond — no kidding. Rewriting takes tons of discipline and practice, but it's what turns a person who happens to put words on paper into a true writer. Some of you might be saying, "But when I write a poem, it comes out fine the first time." Well, maybe. But we bet if you put that "perfect" poem in a drawer for a few months and then look at it again, you'll find something you want to change, whether it's a word, a rhyme, or a comma. Which brings us to the question: How can I critique my own work?

First, it does help to let time pass between drafts, as in

the example above. If you're on some sort of deadline for your writing, you might not have this luxury, but try to take as much time as possible. A rule of thumb is to at least sleep on it! Eventually, with lots of practice, you may be able to revise with shorter and shorter periods of time between drafts.

It's helpful not to get too attached to your first draft. If you think of every word as somehow precious, you'll find it harder to be ruthless in your self-editing, whereas if you remember writing is a *process,* you'll treat your work more like a sculpture you want to keep molding, twisting, and carving into a beautiful shape.

Try breaking down *how* you read your work into several categories before you rewrite. Depending on what kind of piece it is, read once just to weed out unnecessary words (look especially for "lazy" words that don't contribute to your sentences: *very, really, nice*) or substitute better words. Read once for smooth transitions and places you need to clarify or expand. Read once for organization of your thoughts. Read once for grammar, punctuation, and spelling.

After you've written a second draft, try reading your work out loud. Make a mental note of anywhere you stumble or feel awkward. Chances are, that's a place that could use more revision.

Finally, maybe after a third draft, read what you've written again. Does it express what you want it to? The way you want it to? Does it seem like the same person wrote the whole thing, or are there places that are somehow different? Do you get bored anywhere? Is it too long or too short for the subject? Do the kinds of words and images you use seem to fit the topic? Are they too fancy or too ordinary? How would you feel now if someone you respected read this? Are you proud of it? No? Then just remember: it's never too late to write another draft!

Some writers are capable of more drafts than you can imagine. The woman described next believes in the importance of drafts—being able to rewrite has made her a successful published writer.

HIGH PROFILE: SUSANNAH SHEFFER

Susannah Sheffer is the editor of *Growing Without Schooling* magazine, the author of *Writing Because We Love To: Homeschoolers at Work* and *A Sense of Self: Listening to Homeschooled Adolescent Girls,* and a regular columnist for *New Moon Network*.

Susannah has received many requests from young writers for real comments — comments that will improve a piece of their writing. Many girls know when their pieces need improvement and are ready to handle constructive criticism. Susannah tries to respond to them in the same way she would to adult writers.

Susannah tells girls that writing isn't a breeze for adult writers. They, too, go through multiple drafts and have ideas that seem perfect and then don't work out. It is when you're on your tenth draft and still struggling that you're truly a writer, she says.

Many girls write letters to their favorite authors, Susannah observes, but often get only one response. Famous authors can be incredibly busy, and as much as they might love to, they probably don't have the time to correspond with you. Instead, if you want a mentor, try asking adult friends who write to read and comment on your writing.

If they just say, "That's great," and you want more feedback, try someone else. You could exchange stories with a pen pal or ask a friend who writes to look at your work. There are many mentors waiting to be found.

Creating your own writing workshop is another good way to get feedback about your writing. Susannah recommends that you talk about your goals and ways you want to conduct the workshop: do you want to write together during the workshop, or do you want to write separately and bring your pieces to the workshop to be read and commented on by the other members? If you choose to comment on each other's work, remember to be helpful, not hurtful. Constructive comments make a writer want to go and work on her piece instead of making her feel discouraged.

—Caitlin, age 13, Alaska

Let Us Count the Ways . . . to Write

From poetry and plays to short stories and articles, there are many ways to present your ideas in written form. Some writers seem naturally drawn to one genre, such as poetry, while others love to experiment. Now's the time to try a format you've never attempted before. Anyone for a sestina?

Poetry

For some reason, people think that poetry is either sentimental, mushy stuff about flowers and birds and love, or impossible-to-understand code language written to make anyone who reads it feel stupid. These aren't what you would call positive images of this age-old art form, and if you buy into them, you're missing out on a lot. Most good poetry isn't mushy or hard to understand, and yours doesn't have to be, either. Not all poetry rhymes, not all poetry is metered (meaning it has a certain number of syllables per line) or metaphoric, and prose poems aren't even written in lines. Poets pick and choose their words very carefully to try to get a particular response from their readers.

For example:

A: The rain falls hard on my window as I cry.

B: The rain falls soft on my window as I cry.

Don't you get a totally different feeling from each line?

By changing just one word, you create a completely different mood. Writing poetry means you have to be conscious of what you are saying all the time.

Where do you begin to write a poem? A good way to organize your thoughts and words is to use a poetic form. In poetry, a form is a set of rules about the number of lines in a stanza, or the number of syllables or kinds of words in each line. You can even make up your own poetic form! You've probably heard of the sonnet, the fourteen-line form that Shakespeare used—or the haiku, that Japanese form of poetry made up of three lines, each of a certain number of syllables. But what about the sestina, the villanelle, the tanka, and the pantoum? There are dozens of poetic forms. Experimenting with new types is a great way to become a better poet, as you learn to shape your words. Here are some forms you might want to try:

Tanka

This is an ancient form of Japanese poetry, similar to the haiku though much older; the tanka originated as a poetic form *thirteen centuries ago!* A tanka has five lines. The first and third lines consist of five syllables each; lines two, four, and five consist of seven syllables each. Where haiku

33

compares nature and human nature in one concise, concrete image, a tanka focuses more on human emotion by using beautiful lyricism and imagination. Here is an example by Izumi Shikibu, a famous woman poet at the ancient court of the Japanese emperor in the tenth century:

When I think of you,
Fireflies in the marsh rise
Like the soul's jewels,
Lost to eternal longing,
Abandoning my body.

Cinquain

If you don't feel like using a set form, why not make up your own? That's what Adelaide Crapsey did in 1909 when she made up the cinquain form. She had been reading books of Japanese tankas and haiku and decided to invent a new form of five lines (*cinq* means "five" in French). The syllables per line are easy enough to remember: two, four, six, eight, two. The poems are usually unrhymed. Despite how easy it seems to follow, this form hasn't become very popular yet—maybe the world is just waiting for you to come along and take up where Adelaide left off! Here is the most famous example of her cinquains:

TRIAD

These be
Three silent things:
The falling snow...the hour
Before the dawn...the mouth of one
Just dead.

Rhyme or Reason

Sometimes a simple rhyme scheme is enough form for a piece of writing to be considered a poem. A rhyme scheme is a pattern of rhymed lines: for instance, an ABAB rhyme scheme means that the first line rhymes with the third, and the second and fourth lines rhyme with each other. There are tons of different rhyme schemes, and you can always make one up if you don't find one you like. Did you know there are different types of rhymes, too? Annoyingly enough, someone decided to divide rhyme into feminine and masculine categories. A masculine rhyme is words whose final syllables rhyme, in a sort of hard ending — like cat and bat or acrobat and bobcat. And feminine rhyme, the softer kind (is this sexist or what?), is usually the rhyme of the last *two* syllables of words: *revival* and *arrival*, *flutter* and *butter*. If the words at the end of a poem's lines rhyme, this is called end rhyme. But words can also rhyme within the line, which is called internal rhyme: "These are the *years* and the doors and the *tears*." There's also initial rhyme (at the beginning of lines) and cross rhyme (the end of one line with the beginning of the next line). In fact, your words don't even have to rhyme to rhyme! Near, or slant, rhyme is when words almost rhyme or look like they might rhyme (*rain* and a*gain*). So, are you now con*fused* or am*used*?

HIGH PROFILE: NIKKI GIOVANNI

Nikki Giovanni is a well-known poet who has written three books for kids: *Grand Mothers, Shimmy Shimmy Shimmy Like My Sister Kate,* and *The Genie in the Jar.* She is a professor of English at Virginia Tech in Christiansburg, Virginia.

New Moon: When did you decide to become a poet?

Nikki Giovanni: I was really kind of old. I was in college. I thought, "Well, wouldn't it be nice to be a poet?"

NM: What does it mean to be a poet?

NG: I have to observe and look at people and other things and the world in which we live — the floor, and space, and under the sea — because poets are great for looking at everything.

NM: Is being a poet fun?

NG: Yes, it is! I enjoy it, and I think that everybody should write some poetry sometime because it really makes you feel good about yourself.

NM: Did you read a lot of poetry when you were growing up?

NG: I read a lot of everything — poetry, stories, novels, and a lot of history, which I really love. Some plays — not as many plays because I lived in a small town, and we didn't have a theater group. I never got to see plays until I was in high school. The only way that I could "see" a play was to read it.

NM: What do you write about?

NG: I mostly write about people, because they fascinate me. I think they are interesting. We're an interesting species because we're illogical.

NM: How do you get ideas to write poems?

NG: I do a lot of reading. The two most important words for young writers are "Why not?" You need to ask yourself, "Could this happen? Why not?" And then you begin to develop a story or an idea around the why not. You have to be curious. I am always asking myself, "Why not?"

NM: What do you think is easier? Speaking or writing your feelings?

NG: It's about the same thing, isn't it? Isn't writing expressing feelings with words? I will tell you that you can write, because if you can think it and you can say it, then you can write it.

NM: Is there a certain place that you like to write?

NG: I like my own den. I'm comfortable there. I've been writing on this same table for twenty-six years, and I have a rocking chair I've been using for twenty-six years, too. I sit there, and I am very comfortable.

NM: What was your inspiration for writing *The Genie in the Jar*?

NG: I've always been a huge fan of Nina Simone, the singer, and it seemed to me like that was what she was — a genie in a jar. A genius that we didn't really understand. I wanted to write a poem about that.

NM: Which book or poem is your favorite?

NG: That would be like asking me which is my favorite dog, and I have four. I like all of my poems.

—Julia, age 12, Ariel, age 12, and Rebecca, age 11, Minnesota

Letter Writing

Writing letters is a fun and rewarding experience. Letters are an excellent way to keep in touch with people you love and to change the world around you. But they also have hidden benefits for writers.

Writing letters to friends and relatives is a wonderful way to practice your writing, and to express your feelings when you can't see a person face-to-face as often as you want to. Letters are often much more memorable than a conversation on the phone or e-mail. You can save treasured notes forever. You can get creative and personalize your letters by decorating them. Letters can be newsy, romantic, serious, or fun.

Here's an example of a newsy letter:

Dear Lyra,

How are you? I'm good. Okay, here's the update: Cocoa and Feather are fine, I painted my room lime green, one of our turtles died, and Meg is starting school soon. I might be coming out to visit you. I miss you so much! Why on earth did your parents decide to move?!?! Erg.

Anyway, I'm sorry that you're sick. Remember how when one of us was sick, the other would leave a basket full of get-better goodies on their stairs? Tapes, books, candy. Sigh. I'm not an old woman. Why am I sadly reminiscing so much?

Mom's yelling at me to clean my room, so bye!

Love,

Ariel

Letters can also influence companies, and even the government. Many people believe that their letters are discarded and not read, that their hard-worked-on pieces will be ignored. However, this is untrue. A good politician will tell you that her office reads every letter carefully and that letters are often the most powerful influence on someone in the government. As for companies not listening to you, how do you explain Gillette's stopping testing on animals after receiving protest letters? Marketing experts say that companies should figure that for every letter of complaint they get, there are twenty-five more people out there who are mad, too, but who have never bothered to write!

The pen is mightier than the sword. Use your weapon well.

Journal

A journal is a great way to express yourself through writing. Keeping a journal is a hard habit to maintain, though. Make yourself write in it at least once a week. It doesn't have to include every detail of your life, but it is a place where you can say how you are feeling, what you are thinking about, and what your goals are. By writing in a journal, you are not only able to vent your frustrations, you are recording your life. A journal preserves your memories and emotions in ways that a picture or even a video can't.

Have a journal with you when you travel. Record all your memories of places you may never visit again. Record all your experiences, smells, sights, the people you encounter, and other impressions you have. Keeping a journal can help your fiction writing by providing material. For example, your trip to Jamaica could provide terrific ideas, details, and dialogue for a story, but only if you write them down. It also forces you to practice writing, and practice makes progress!

Did You Know?

Many writers choose to keep journals or use notebooks to record ideas they have. Susannah Sheffer says that this can be a good idea as long as you are keeping a journal because you want to, not because a parent or teacher tells you to. Feeling guilty about not writing and apologizing to your journal are ridiculous if you are writing in it for yourself.

Short Stories and Novels

Within the huge world known as fiction are many countries. Will you decide to write an allegory, a fable, a fairy tale, a fantasy, a legend, a mystery, a myth, a romance, or historical or science fiction? Once you know, you can work on the building blocks of writing fiction. Without a strong foundation, your work is likely to crumble and fall.

Plot

The plot is the scheme or plan of things, otherwise known as the story itself. The plot is what happens to give the story its action. In the fairy tale "Sleeping Beauty," the plot is that an evil fairy casts a spell over a castle so that all of its inhabitants sleep. A prince comes and kisses Sleeping Beauty, which awakens all from their slumber.

Writers sometimes use an outline to help organize what they want to happen. Then they take all the stuff they outlined and turn it into a story. The story needs characters, a setting, and a beginning, a middle, and an end. Most good plots have a point near the end called the *climax*. This is the high point of the whole story, the most dramatic moment, the event that the whole plot has been leading up to.

Usually, a climax is followed by the *denouement*, which is the story's end. The author ties up the plot in the denouement, also called the *resolution*.

Character

Without characters there would be no story. You already know the five W's (*Who? What? Where? When? Why?*). The character (or characters) is the Who. A character is a person or being in your story. It can be a girl or a boy, a man or a woman, a mouse or a robot, a dragon or an ant or even an alien, good or evil. The main character is the one the story follows, or the most important. For example, in the nursery rhyme "Mary Had a Little Lamb," Mary is the main character. A well-written character should have believable emotions. The main character doesn't necessarily have to be "good," but it helps if the reader is able to sympathize with her or him.

You need to describe your characters. That way the reader can relate to them. You can name them, include what they look like, and make them talk. Here's an example:

Cindy walked down the street to her best friend Julie's
house. Her blond hair blew in the breeze, and her brown

eyes sparkled. That was when she caught sight of red-headed Julie. Smiling, she waved and called out, "Hi, Julie!"

Doesn't Cindy seem cheerful and happy in this short scene? Notice that the writer didn't *tell* you that her character was in a good mood. She *showed* you by providing clues: Cindy's eyes "sparkled," she was "smiling," she "called out, 'Hi, Julie!'" That's more interesting to read than "Cindy was feeling happy."

Characters can live and die. They can be whoever you want them to be. Just use your imagination.

Dialogue

In fiction, good dialogue moves the plot along, develops your characters, and gives the readers a break, a refreshing pause, so they want to keep reading. Bad dialogue can do the opposite of all these things and turn your story to rags. Learning the difference between good dialogue and bad dialogue and how to write it can take a long time. Good dialogue sounds natural, meaning the reader can believe that your character actually would say whatever you've written. This also depends on the character, of course. Each character should have his or her own unique voice and should speak a certain way, with the words you would expect him or her to use (in literary terms this is called *diction*).

For dialogue to sound natural, you need to know how normal speech flows. It doesn't seem as if it would be that hard, since you speak the English language every day, but often when you try to re-create speech on the page, it comes out sounding weird and awkward. To get better at this, eavesdrop on people's conversations and really listen to how their conversation flows; then imagine how their words would look on the printed page.

It is always a good idea to read your dialogue *out loud* to yourself while you are writing it and again when you are done — your ear will pick up the weak or awkward spots in the dialogue, and you will be able to fix them. Sounding natural is very important, but getting your meaning across clearly is equally important. This usually means being concise and paying attention to your language in much the same way you have to when writing poetry. You've probably noticed that when people talk, they inject a lot of unnecessary words into their speech, like "like," "um," "and," "uh," and "you know," you know? Putting these into your fictional dialogue slows it down too much and quickly bores the reader. Even introductory phrases like "I was thinking," "You know what?" and "Well..." can have this effect. The best dialogue cuts to the chase and gives the reader information in every sentence, every clause — strive for this and you'll "sound" good in print.

Setting

Wherever your story takes place is the setting. It can be the past or the future, on this planet or in outer space, in the real world or on an imaginary island. You can have the most interesting characters and the smoothest dialogue out there, but without establishing the setting, something is still missing — the details, the scenery, the *imagery*. Notice the root of that word: image. You need to create an image in your readers' minds, or all your hard work will be in vain. Never fear, you are fully equipped with everything required to do this: your five senses. Nothing creates a picture in someone's mind like sensory images — how something smells or looks or tastes or feels or sounds. Try to work two or three senses into each descriptive passage. Say you're describing the meadow where your main character is walking: How does it look? Are there flowers? What

47

kind? What color is the sky? What color is the grass? Can your character feel the grass under her feet or brushing her arms? Is there a warm breeze on her neck? Does the grass make a swishing sound when the wind blows, and are there bees buzzing around her head? Does the earth smell like clay or rain or dirt, and does it taste sandy when it gets blown into her mouth?

Do you get the picture? Good. Your reader will, too!

HIGH PROFILE: MADELEINE L'ENGLE

Madeleine L'Engle has fascinated several generations of children and adults with her books, including *A Wrinkle in Time, A Swiftly Tilting Planet,* and *A Wind in the Door*.

New Moon: Did your imagination ever get you in trouble?

Madeleine L'Engle: Heavens, yes! Once I was in boarding school and I pretended that I had a twin brother in England. We had a correspondence going between my English twin brother and one of my classmates. And when she found out he wasn't real, I was in big trouble.

NM: What happened?

ML: Everybody was very mad at me for a while. I said,

"But it was just a game!" They finally forgave me. Problem was, one of the girls fell in love with my twin brother who didn't exist. You have to watch your imagination.

NM: Where do you get your ideas?

ML: Once upon a time, when the great composer Johann Sebastian Bach was an old man, a student asked him, "Bach, where did you get the ideas for all these melodies?" The old man said, "Well, when I get up in the morning, it's all I can do not to trip over them." That's just how it is. Ideas are everywhere.

NM: Of all your books, which do you like best?

ML: That's like asking which of my children I like best. I love them all. In a way, *A Wrinkle in Time* is special because it almost never got published. You can't name a publisher who didn't reject it. They didn't know who the book was for. They said, "Is this book for children? Is this book for grownups?" I said, "It's for people. Don't *people* read books?" When my present publishers finally bought it, they took me out to lunch and said, "Now, dear, we don't want you to be disappointed; this book is not going to sell, because it is too difficult for children. We're just

49

doing it because we like it." They were very surprised when it became a bestseller.

NM: In your books, you describe going inside a person, and lights and stuff. Where did you get that?

ML: Well, I guess from learning physics and quantum mechanics. The world is infinitely small and infinitely large, and basically it doesn't make much difference if we're big or little. And the ideas sort of all come together as I look at my characters. I think while I'm writing, rather than before.

NM: Do you still read children's books?

ML: Of course! Some of the best books are written for children because the writer knows perfectly well that adults can't manage them. If I have something to say that I think is going to be too hard for the grown-up world, I will use a young protagonist.

NM: When did you start writing?

ML: I wrote my first story when I was five, and it was about a little g-r-u-l, because that was how I spelled "girl" when I was five. I began writing because I think that if you want to know the truth about life — why people do what they do, why there's war, why people hurt each other, why people love each other—you turn to stories, not encyclopedias. That's where we find out who we are. Writing a story is listening to the story. Most writers of fiction will agree our characters do things we don't expect them to, they say things we didn't plan for them to say. And they know better than we do, and we have to listen to them.

NM: Do you have a character in one of your books that you think of as you?

ML: All of my major characters are me. Meg is me. I made her good at arithmetic and bad at English, and I was good at English and bad at arithmetic. I was an only child, so I gave her three brothers. That's the kind of thing you can do in fiction.

NM: Do you like to take different characters from different books and weave them together into a new story?

ML: I love to do that. I did that first with *Dragons in the Waters* when I introduced characters from *The Arm of the Starfish* to characters from *The Young Unicorns*. It was a lot of fun.

NM: Do you have any advice for girl writers?

ML: My advice to anybody, male or female, about writing

51

is very simple. It's three things. One is to keep an honest, unpublishable journal that you don't show anybody. It's yours; you're writing your own story. And then read. You can't be a good writer if you're not a good reader. And then write.

—Nia, age 14, Marit, age 11, and Amanda, age 10, Minnesota

The Play's the Thing

You can write short, one-act plays or longer plays with two or three acts. Each act may have more than one scene, especially if there needs to be a change of costumes, props, or sets. When you write a play, you use many of the ideas we've already mentioned — plot, character, dialogue. But there are two big differences between a play and a story. First, in a play you have to depend completely on dialogue to convey the plot and the characters. Second, because a play is meant to be acted out on a stage, you have to write stage directions, or what you want your characters to do while they're onstage, as well as what you want them to say.

You can suggest how you want your characters to look by describing them in as much detail as you want in stage directions. You can also describe props and sets. For example, this is how the beginning of one play would look in written form:

> *Act I, Scene i:* Mara is sitting at a desk, writing furiously. Her mother quietly enters, crossing from stage left to behind Mara. She waits until Mara realizes she's there.
>
> *Mother:* Oh, Mara, it's such a beautiful day. Can't you get outside now and work on your story later?
>
> *Mara (grinning):* You know, most parents would kill for a kid who likes to write as much as I do!

Notice that the Roman numeral for the act is capitalized and the one for the scene is lowercase. The actual dialogue is written after the character's name and a colon. To write your own play, start with a general idea of what you want it to be about. Write an outline that includes a plot, a description of the characters, and the set. Then write a rough draft that focuses on the actions and the general idea of what each character says. Later you can go back and polish the dialogue and give more accurate stage directions.

In playwriting, reading aloud is a must. Find as many friends or relatives as you need to do a reading while you take notes and decide what lines you'd like to change.

If you're really lucky, maybe you'll get your play produced. Break a leg!

Writing Roundup

Poems, plays, stories, novels, letters, journals — what else can a girl write? Plenty! Sometimes our most creative genres aren't necessarily those we first think of as "creative" writing. You'll know what we're talking about if you've ever read great examples of the following kinds of writing:

Personal essays. In a first-person essay, you are not only the writer, you are the "speaker." You can voice an opinion on anything — pets, hobbies, relationships, politics — you name it!

Book reviews. You can review your favorite novels and also nonfiction books. Keep in mind that a good review does much more than summarize the book; it evaluates how effective the book is in what the author set out to do.

Newspaper and magazine articles. Articles need to get right to the point and include the basic information a reader would need to understand the person, the crime, the election, the accident, the achievement, the discovery — whatever the article is about.

Travelogues. Have you ever read a description of a place that was so vivid you felt as if you were there? Or that you couldn't wait to go there? That's the purpose of a travel piece.

Letters to the editor. Magazines and newspapers often print readers' reactions to articles from their publications or to the world in general.

Not only does experimenting with different forms help you figure out whether or not you like to write in those genres, it almost always improves your more traditional "creative" writing. Some of the best novelists in the world, for example, started out as journalists, where they learned to observe carefully and to be concise. Writing travelogues can help your descriptions of settings in short stories. Personal essays can sharpen your organizational skills, which in turn can help you develop great plots.

If you're inspired to take a whack at these types of

writing, we suggest you first look through magazines and newspapers at the library to discover hundreds of essays, articles on travel, and reviews. The opinion/editorial page of your local newspaper usually carries letters to the editor. After you've gotten familiar with various styles and genres, you can try writing your own pieces. Also, check the resources chapter (page 71) for many books on various kinds of writing.

Fun with Writing

CHAPTER FOUR

We've rounded up games, crafts, projects, and quizzes for your writing-related pleasure. Enjoy a few, or try them all!

Decorating Letters

There are a lot of things you can do to make letters to people special. You can cut your writing paper into shapes or put stickers on the envelope. If you have a computer, you can design stationery with computer graphics. There are books on how to make homemade paper with flowers and recycled paper. You can also make collages of magazine clippings or old postage stamps on the back of your letter. You can write your letter in calligraphy. You can doodle around the edges of the paper or even burn the edges of the paper so it looks worn and antique (have an adult help you, stay near the sink, and don't burn the house down, okay?). You can paint with watercolors on the stationery and then write on top of the painting. There are millions of things you can do to snazz up your letters, making them more fun to read. You just have to use your imagination.

Calligraphy

Calligraphy is the ancient art of writing in a beautiful style using certain kinds of letters. The word comes from *kalligraphia*—Greek for "beautiful handwriting." Before the invention of the printing press, calligraphy was used in all books to illuminate, or decorate, borders, margins, and the first letter of a page.

Today, it's fun to use calligraphy to make special birthday cards, invitations, stationery, diaries, notebooks—anything you can write on. First, it is a good idea to buy a special pen and ink from an art supply store. You will probably need a book to show you how to form the letters. One we like, especially good for beginners, is *Calligraphy Project Workstation* by Manda Hanson (Price Stern Sloan, 1993). If you want to conserve money, check out calligraphy books from the library.

Calligraphy takes a lot of practice. Getting the ink to flow right, for example, is a skill you'll need to master before you can create calligraphic work you're happy with. But there are "flow" exercises to help you do just that, so be patient with yourself and enjoy the process!

Creative Bookmarks

Bookmarks are for marking your place in a book. Now, you could just use a boring old piece of paper, or (drumroll,

59

please…) you could create a beautiful, quirky, original, or funny work of art to keep your place in a special book. There are many kinds you can make: sticker-covered, doodled-on, pressed flower (cut a piece of sturdy white cardboard, arrange flowers on it, cover them with contact paper), or scratch art (cover a piece of thin cardboard with bright colors, using oil pastels, crayons, or paint; paint over the colors with lots of layers of black; and, using a sharp object, carefully scratch away the layer of black, drawing flowers, stars, people — whatever you want). Or simply draw a picture on a piece of paper. There now, wasn't that satisfying?

—Flynn, age 11, New York

(*Editors' note:* If you want to try a more elaborate kind of bookmark, you can order a Beaded Bookmark Kit from a crafts catalog called Lark Books at 800-284-3388.)

Lit Quiz

How much do you know about women and girls in literature? *Hint:* Some of the answers are in this book! You can also find them on page 86.

1. What was George Eliot's real name?

2. What book by L. M. Montgomery was rejected five times by five different publishers before it was sold?

3. Who wrote Newbery Medal–winning *Walk Two Moons*?

4. How old was S. E. Hinton when she wrote *The Outsiders*?

5. What character in *Little Women* represented Louisa May Alcott?

6. What author wrote *Their Eyes Were Watching God*?

7. In *The Diary of Latoya Hunter*, was Latoya Hunter starting high school or junior high?

8. Who was the first published African American poet?

9. Who wrote *Dicey's Song*?

10. How many girls are on the editorial board for New Moon Books?

—Elizabeth, age 12, New Jersey

A Friendship Journal

It's cool to have a special bond with your close friends. Writing notes to each other is always fun. So why not make a *note*book full of them? You can find a special book to write in and have each person write in a certain color. You write a message, and then your friend writes back. You can add little things that remind you of times together. You can add decorative things, like stickers or cool Band-Aids. When my friend and I made a friendship book, we added sticker photos we had taken together. We also added pictures we had taken at a friend's birthday party. We did collages and lots of other things. You can add quotes or poems you both like, too. We had two identical books going at the same time so that we would both end up with one to keep.

—Lauren, age 13, Hawaii

POINT OF VIEW: *Producing a Play*

The Birch Play, or *A Tale from Hidden Valley*, as we later came to call it, started as a story about the adventures of Birch (a young chipmunk), Dandelion (a beautiful squirrel), and Chestnut-Bone (a tough, feisty red squirrel). My group of homeschoolers wrote it section-by-section, passing them by hand and mail over distances as far as fifty miles. When it was done, we all felt so absorbed in the story that we wanted to act it out. So we decided to make it into a play. Three of us rewrote the story, using most of the original dialogue with some additions because we had to cut out the descriptions. The story worked well as a play because it had a simple, understandable plot and not too many parts.

Since we had written and edited the play ourselves, we already knew the play so well that it wasn't hard to memorize the lines. We did have to work out the blocking, though—that is, how the actors move around the stage—and since we could only meet once a week, it took us quite a while to get it down. It was a challenge to get anything done at rehearsals, since everybody had different ideas and told the rest of us about them very loudly. It was great to all work together, though, and doing the play gave our group a real sense of teamwork.

With help from our parents, we designed our own costumes, props, and sets. They were simple but effective. All we had for sets were two cardboard boulders that we colored with chalk. So we created the character of the Artist to describe the setting at the beginning of each scene.

We wrote a letter to the director of our local theater and gained permission to use it for one of our productions at no cost as long as we didn't charge admission. Our second production we did at one of the local schools and adapted the play so that the school kids could be in it, too. At the theater, we got a kid to do the lights, so kids did almost everything. We wrote and illustrated our own programs, and even wrote lyrics for a song to the tune of "Good King Wenceslaus" and got one of the parents to accompany us on piano!

We learned a lot of things from doing the play, like if you have black-painted noses and a black backdrop, when you turn sideways it looks like you have no nose at all. Also, we think that maybe next time we'll put an ad on the radio or in the newspaper instead of just inviting friends. But on the whole, I think it was one of the best things our group has done. Yet.

—Caitlin, age 13, Alaska

Words, Words, Words

There's no end to ways to have fun just exploring words, from browsing in a dictionary for exotic, unfamiliar, or pretty words to learning all about the history of slang. No matter what you're interested in, there are specialized references to find out more. Look up synonyms in a thesaurus, definitions of writing terms in a manual of style, and the history of language in the *Oxford English Dictionary*. Find cool quotes in books with indexed quotations and proverbs. There are crossword dictionaries, Scrabble dictionaries, dictionaries of misunderstood and mispronounced words — even a dictionary of clichés, which you can use to avoid them in your own writing! All these delicious books are only a library away.

Mad Libs

Mad Libs is a fun word game, especially great for those long car trips. You can buy Mad Libs, of course, but did you ever consider making them up? That can be as much fun as playing the game! All you have to do is find a short story or description — or write one yourself. Next, go through it, and in each sentence cross out a noun, a verb, and an adjective or an adverb. Write above it what kind of word you're crossing out: noun, verb, adjective, etc. Whenever you come to a place marked "noun," "verb," etc., ask your friends to think of an example of that part of speech and jot it down. When you're done, read the story out loud with the "new" nouns, verbs, etc. We guarantee you'll be rolling on the ground laughing.

Follow the Bouncing Ball

Get a bunch of friends together, grab a rubber ball, and stand in a circle. Decide on a subject, like kinds of transportation, then throw the ball to a player. The player has to name a kind of transportation. Then she throws the ball to someone else, who has to say a kind of transportation that hasn't been used yet. As more words get used up, the game gets harder and harder.

—Ashley, age 10, Minnesota

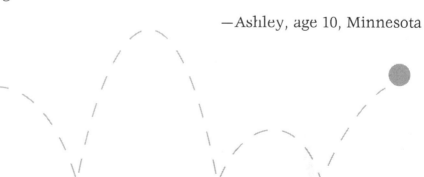

Did You Know?

Russian kids use a secret language called Ku. The syllable "ku" is put in front of each syllable. "Farmers in Russia grow large amounts of wheat, barley, corn, and cherries" would be "Ku-farm ku-ers ku-in ku-rus ku-sia ku-grow ku-large ku-a ku-mounts ku-of ku-wheat, ku-bar ku-ley, ku-corn, ku-and ku-cher ku-ries."

A secret language from China is called Sa-La. To speak Sa-La, each syllable is repeated three times: the first time, the syllable is said correctly; the second time, it starts with the letter "s"; the third time, it starts with the letter "l." The new syllables are pronounced so that they rhyme with the original syllable. "China was the first country to have a population of more than one billion" would be "Chin-sin-lin a-sa-la was-sas-las the-se-le first-sirst-lirst coun-soun-loun try-sy-ly to-so-lo have-save-lave a-sa-la pop-sop-lop u-su-lu la-sa-la tion-sion-lion of-sof-lof more-sore-lore than-san-lan one-sone-lone bil-sil-lil lion-sion-lion."

Le Papier

Have you ever seen Japanese rice paper? How about rag paper? There are as many different kinds of paper available as there are different kinds of girls! Experiment with marbleized, tissue, construction, cotton, and cardstock paper. You can even try writing on wallpaper or wrapping paper!

If you get really ambitious and have a free Saturday afternoon, you can make your own paper. Here's a recipe for papermaking from Julia, 14:

 **Materials**

10 sheets of newspaper

Large pot

2 cups water

Blender, egg beater, or spoon

Deep pan

2 tablespoons liquid starch or stiffener

Piece of nylon or plastic screen (about 5" x 10")

Additional sheets of newspaper, for blotting

Jar, bottle, or rolling pin

 How to Make Paper

1. Tear the 10 sheets of newspaper into very small pieces and place them in large pot.

2. Pour in water. Let the mixture sit for a few hours, until paper is soggy.

3. Blend water and soggy paper in blender in small amounts, or mix them thoroughly with egg beater or spoon. The mixture, or pulp, should have the consistency of oatmeal.

4. Pour pulp into pan and add starch. Stir about three minutes.

5. Slide screen under pulp. Move screen around until pulp covers half of screen. Pulp should be $1/8$" thick.

6. Lift screen out carefully. Hold it level and let it drain about one minute.

7. Fold other half of screen over pulp and place it on several layers of newspaper. Put more newspaper on top.

8. Roll jar, bottle, or rolling pin over newspaper to squeeze rest of water out.

9. Take off top layers of newspaper. Remove pulp from folded screen. It will be paper!

10. Let recycled paper dry overnight before you write on it.

Hint: Handmade paper makes a truly unique and beautiful gift, either with a special message written on it or left blank.

Finding Out More About Writing

CHAPTER FIVE

Part One:

Publish if you can, but don't perish if you can't!

If you think you want to find places to be published, this is easier than you might guess. For instance, doesn't your school have a newspaper or publication that prints kids' work? How about your town newspaper? Check your library bulletin board, Web sites, and, of course, the resources in Part Two for magazines and contests looking for good writing. Read a few issues of the publication to get a feel for what they publish.

When you've written something you think is ready to submit, check first with the publication for its submission guidelines so you'll know how to format your piece. Editors, who have to read thousands of words, can be very picky about what they'll accept. You don't want to eliminate your chance to be published by making their jobs harder or ignoring their rules.

Here are some general guidelines:

1. This rule is set in stone: Your work *must* be original. As in *you and only you wrote every bit of it by yourself.*
2. It's best to type (or print extremely clearly in blue or black ink only) on 8½" x 11" sheets of white paper. Use only one side of each sheet.

3. Be sure to include your name, address, phone number, and e-mail address on your manuscript.

4. Number the pages.

5. Include a self-addressed, stamped envelope, known in the publishing biz as an SASE.

6. Proofread at *least* three times yourself and also ask someone else to proofread! And no smudges, soda stains, rips, etc.

7. Keep a copy of your work — many publications don't return submissions.

8. Good luck!

If you are at all serious about your writing and begin to submit it on a regular basis, you'll want to set up some kind of tracking or record-keeping system. When she was 14, famous nature writer Rachel Carson started a ledger for the stories and articles she sent out to newspapers and magazines. She used the same format her whole writing life. Here's what it looked like:

Name	Class	Length	Where submitted	Date sent	Date returned	Paid	Comments
"Just Dogs"	Short story	4,000 words	*Authors' Press*	July 14, 1921	July 31, 1921		
			St. Nicholas	Aug. 1	Aug. 21		

This entry from Rachel's journal shows what happened to a story called "Just Dogs," which she wrote in 1921 and sent off to two different children's magazines. "Just Dogs" was returned, or rejected, by both magazines. But Rachel was not discouraged. She matter-of-factly recorded the dates the story was returned. She didn't write a comment for this story because the editors didn't find anything wrong with it. They simply couldn't use it because they already had a great many dog stories. By the time Rachel was 15, she had received several awards and payments for her stories.

POINT OF VIEW: *Contests*

When I was 10, I sent a chapter about writing to a contest in *New Moon*. Later, I got a call that told me I was going to be published in a book called *Girls Know Best*. I was so excited. It was a hard process that took an extremely long time. I did a TV interview and a newspaper interview, not to mention three book signings. I encourage any girl who loves to write to enter contests. You never know what could happen!

—Katie, age 11, Minnesota

Getting Published: From A to 'Zines

There's a new-fashioned, popular way to publish your writing, and it's available to any girl. A 'zine, short for "fanzine," which in turn is a combination of the words "fanatic" and "magazine," is a short magazine on paper or on the Web on whatever subject the author feels like writing about. It has no advertising and does not circulate very widely (its audience may be in the tens or the hundreds). There were more than 10,000 very varied 'zines out there last time we looked.

'Zines do not have to be, or look, cheap. There are a lot of very high-quality ones, in fact. There are 'zines on feminism, movies, dreams, anarchy, art, mysteries, how it's cool to be a dork, comics, music, interior design, autobiography, aliens, writing, and much more. 'Zines are as varied as the people who make them. To sample some 'zines, get a copy of *Factsheet Five*, a magazine that reviews 'zines, or the book *Zine Scene* by Francesca Lia Block and Hillary Carlip. *The Millennium Whole Earth Catalog* has a few wonderful pages on 'zines, too. If you order one 'zine, it will probably list other good 'zines. So you can keep getting more and more, if you want.

It's simple to make a 'zine: type or legibly handwrite

whatever it is you want to say, print it (if you used a computer), lay it out and perhaps arrange graphics around it (magazines are great sources for graphics…get out the scissors!), photocopy it, and send off copies to friends, family, other 'zines that review 'zines, *Factsheet Five*, and whomever else you can think of. Wait for orders to come in and fulfill them. There now, that was easy!

Part Two:
Resources

A comprehensive list of resources for the New Moon girl who'd like to keep exploring and having fun with writing.

Print Publications

The following publications accept submissions from kids and teens:

NEW MOON
P.O. Box 3587
Duluth, MN 55803-3587

Accepts fiction and nonfiction up to 900 words; personal essays, profiles, and interviews with girls and women; science, math, and craft activities; and poetry. Check writer's guidelines at www.newmoon.org/nmgirl/gguide.html.

AGORA
Thomas E. Humble and Sally R. Humble, Editors
AG Publications
P.O. Box 10975
Raleigh, NC 27605-0975

Accepts fiction up to 3,000 words, one-act plays under 20 minutes, and nonfiction up to 2,500 words.

CREATIVE WITH WORDS
Brigitta Geltrich, Editor
P.O. Box 223226
Carmel, CA 93922

Accepts fiction and nonfiction up to 1,000 words. Request guidelines for theme list.

HOW ON EARTH!
Sally Clinton, Editor
Vegetarian Education Network
P.O. Box 339
Oxford, PA 19363-0339

Accepts fiction and nonfiction, word count varies. Also puzzles, games, jokes, and poetry.

KIDS' WORLD JOURNAL
Nancy Bell, Editor
P.O. Box 389-C, Route 3
Rocky Mount, VA 24151

Accepts fiction, 300 to 500 words, as well as puzzles, games, jokes, and activities from kids.

THE McGUFFEY WRITER

Mary Fuller, Children's Editor
P.O. Box 502
Oxford, OH 45056-0502

Accepts fiction and nonfiction up to 500 words. Also activities and puzzles, and poetry up to 30 lines.

MERLYN'S PEN

R. James Stahl, Editor
P.O. Box 1058
East Greenwich, RI 02818
E-mail: merlynspen@aol.com

Accepts fiction and nonfiction up to 3,000 words. Before e-mailing the editors at *Merlyn's Pen,* go to the Web site at **merlynspen.com** for complete information. Authors contributing to *Merlyn's Pen* must first have a copy of Merlyn's Official Cover Sheet for Submissions, which you can download from **merlynspen.com**.

STONE SOUP

Gerry Mandel, Editor
Children's Art Foundation
P.O. Box 83
Santa Cruz, CA 95063-0083

Accepts book reviews, poetry, and fiction from writers aged 13 and under.

TEEN VOICES

P.O. Box 6329 JFK
Boston, MA 02114

Accepts fiction and nonfiction up to 400 words, games, activities, and jokes from girls 12 to 20 years old.

WINDCHIME
70 Raymond Hts.
Petaluma, CA 94952

Accepts short stories, poems, essays, articles, and book reviews written by teens.

Books (Nonfiction)

We've divided the nonfiction book section into three parts. The first part, "General and Genres," includes books on writing, writers, and specific kinds of writing (journals, poetry, etc.). The second part, "Publishing," contains guides to getting published. The third part, "Reference," lists books that every writer, young or old, should have in her library.

General and Genres

The Art of Making Comic Books by Michael Pellowski (Lerner Publications, 1995)

Blood on the Forehead: What I Know About Writing by M. E. Kerr (HarperCollins, 1998)

A Book of Your Own: Keeping a Diary or Journal by Carla Stevens (Clarion, 1993)

Careers for Wordsmiths (Choices) by Andrew Kaplan (Millbrook Press, 1991)

Creative Nonfiction: How to Live It and Write It by Lee Gutkind (John Wiley, 1997)

A Crow Doesn't Need a Shadow: A Guide to Writing Poetry from Nature by Lorraine Ferra, illustrated by Diane Boardman (Gibbs Smith, 1994)

How to Write a Poem (Speak Out, Write On) by Margaret Ryan (Franklin Watts, 1996)

Knock at a Star: A Child's Introduction to Poetry compiled by X. J. Kennedy and Dorothy M. Kennedy (Little, Brown, 1985)

On Writing Well: An Informal Guide to Writing Nonfiction by William Knowlton Zinsser (out of print)

Poetry from A to Z: A Guide for Young Writers by Paul B. Janeczko (Atheneum, 1994)

Totally Private & Personal: Journaling Ideas for Girls and Young Women by Jessica Wilber (Free Spirit, 1996)

What Do Authors Do? by Eileen Christelow (Clarion, 1995)

What's Your Story? A Young Person's Guide to Writing Fiction by Marion Dane Bauer (Clarion, 1992)

Writing Because We Love To: Homeschoolers at Work by Susannah Sheffer (Heinemann, 1992)

Writing Down the Days: 365 Creative Journaling Ideas for Young People by Lorraine M. Dahlstrom (Free Spirit, 1990)

Writing Personal Essays: How to Shape Your Life Experiences for the Page by Sheila Bender (Writers Digest, 1995)

Writing with Style by Sue Young (Scholastic, 1997)

Publishing

Freed's Guide to Student Contests and Publishing by Judith Freed (Fountainpen Press, 1994)

Market Guide for Young Writers: Where and How to Sell What You Write by Kathy Henderson (Writers Digest, 1998)

Rising Voices: A Guide to Young Writers' Resources (Poets & Writers, 1997)

To Be a Writer: A Guide for Young People Who Want to Write and Publish by Barbara Seuling (Twenty First Century Books, 1997)

The Young Author's Do-It-Yourself Book: How to Write, Illustrate, and Produce Your Own Book by Donna Guthrie, Nancy Bentley, and Katy Keck Arnsteen (Millbrook Press, 1994)

The Young Journalist's Book: How to Write and Produce Your Own Newspaper by Nancy Bentley, et al. (Millbrook Press, 1998)

Zine Scene: The Do It Yourself Guide to Zines by Francesca Lia Block and Hillary Carlip (Girl Press, 1998)

Reference

The American Heritage Dictionary of the English Language, 3rd edition (Houghton Mifflin, 1992)

The American Heritage Dictionary of Idioms edited by Christine Ammer (Houghton Mifflin, 1997)

The Chicago Manual of Style: The Essential Guide for Writers, Editors, and Publishers, 14th edition (University of Chicago Press, 1993)

The Dictionary of Clichés by James Rogers (Ballantine Books, 1987)

Dictionary of Word Origins: A History of the Words, Expressions, and Clichés We Use by Jordan Almond (Citadel Press, 1995)

The Elements of Style, 4th edition, by William Strunk, Jr., and E. B. White (Allyn & Bacon, 1999)

Familiar Quotations edited by John Bartlett (Little, Brown, 1968)

The Merriam-Webster Dictionary of Synonyms and Antonyms (Merriam-Webster, 1992)

Merriam-Webster's Collegiate Dictionary, 10th edition (Merriam-Webster, 1998)

The New Shorter Oxford English Dictionary edited by Lesley Brown (Oxford University Press, 1993)

The Oxford Dictionary of Quotations edited by Angela Partington (Oxford University Press, 1996)

Random House Historical Dictionary of American Slang edited by J. E. Lighter (Random House, 1997)

Roget's International Thesaurus edited by Robert L. Chapman (Harper-Collins, 1992)

Wired Style: Principles of English Usage in the Digital Age by Constance Hale (Hardwired, 1997)

Books (Fiction and Poetry)

Daphne's Book by Mary Downing Hahn (Houghton Mifflin, 1983)

Emily of New Moon by L. M. Montgomery (Bantam Doubleday Dell, 1998)

Harriet the Spy by Louise Fitzhugh (HarperCollins, 1987)

Libby on Wednesday by Zilpha Keatley Snyder (Yearling Books, 1991)

Muggie Maggie by Beverly Cleary (William Morrow, 1990)

A Ring of Endless Light by Madeleine L'Engle (Farrar, Straus & Giroux, 1980)

Ten-Second Rainshowers: Poems by Young People edited by Sandford Lyne (Simon & Schuster, 1996)

Internet

www.newmoon.org

The inside scoop on *New Moon,* with stories from the magazine, contests, and other fun interactive features. Also, tips for how to start and run your own New Moon Writing Club or Reading Club

www.asahi-net.or.jp/~JN2K-srmz/haiku/top.html

The Haiku Exchange Project allows school classes in different countries to share their best haiku writing on this site.

www.TheCase.com/kids/writing
Mystery-writing contest.

www.girlpower.com
Featuring personal writing by young teenage girls.

www.inkspot.com/young
The Inkspot: For Young Writers page links to plenty of useful information for young authors, including advice and markets for selling your work.

www.kidpub.org
This site allows kids to read stories written by other kids and to submit their own for online publication.

www.mystworld.com/youngwriter/index.html
A place for kids aged 6 to 16 to share their creative-writing endeavors.

www.realkids.com/club.shtml
True-life stories of kids who have had very interesting adventures. Television's Discovery Channel airs film of some of these adventures on the weekly series of the same name. Site features include: "Story Room," "Young Writers," "Ask the Author," "Teacher's Lounge," "Clubhouse," and intriguing film shots from the television series.

www.smartgirl.com
Reviews of books by girls for girls.

www.stonesoup.com
Web site for the journal *Stone Soup*. Includes creative writing and art for and by children all over the world.

www.teenvoices.com
An online magazine written by and for young women, with articles that challenge traditional gender stereotypes, as well as a chat room.

www.worddance.com
Letters, field trips, haiku, interesting links, writing tips, and more.

www.ypp.net
Young People's Press Online accepts opinion pieces, news stories, and features from contributors aged 14 to 24. Read pieces from other teens about music, race, art, and many other issues.

www.zuzu.org
Zuzu welcomes young artists, photographers, and writers to contribute their creative work. Highlights include "My Neighborhood" and "My Collection," which invite kids to write about their hometowns and their hobby collections.

E-'Zines for Young Writers

www.asonline.net/utterance/index.html
Utterance Magazine

spectr.com/sbm.html
Surrounded by Morons

Writing Instruction

www.dimax.com/pif/chronicl.htm
Chronicles of Fiction is an online prose-writing workshop. Read other people's work and submit your own work for display.

www.grammarlady.com
Log on to get any grammar question answered by a funny lady who knows what she's talking about.

jhunix.hcf.jhu.edu/~ewt2
Center for Talented Youth Writing Tutorials describes the tutorials available via e-mail and CD-ROM from Johns Hopkins University for qualifying young writers, as well as providing information for parents and teachers and links to other pages useful to young writers.

webster.commnet.edu/HP/pages/darling/grammar.htm
Learn how to write effective paragraphs and essays in addition to finding out about all things grammatical. You can even submit a question about English grammar or usage. Lots of resources available, too, including an online dictionary and famous quotations about writing.

Answers to quiz on pages 60–61

1. Mary Ann Evans

2. *Anne of Green Gables*

3. Sharon Creech

4. Sixteen years old

5. Jo March

6. Zora Neale Hurston

7. Junior high school

8. Phillis Wheatley

9. Cynthia Voigt

10. Nine girls

Hi! My name is *Flynn Berry*. I'm 11 years old and live in a barely there, tiny teeny little speck-on-the-map suburb of New York City, New York. I love to write and create any form of art (collages, paintings, drawings, etc.). I am also interested in helping humans, including myself, stop hurting animals; playing soccer; karate; playing the flute; reading (particularly any Philip Pullman books, and anything by Madeleine L'Engle); exploring New York City; and spending time with my friends.

My name is *Lauren Noelani Calhoun,* and I am 13 years old. I live on the island of Kauai, Hawaii. I enjoy cooking, playing the oboe, hiking and camping, dancing, running, and spending time with friends. I have a service club called the Kids Helping Kids Club and volunteer at a women's shelter. I baby-sit whenever I get a chance, and I am learning to cook with a chef in a local restaurant. I hope to be a chef when I grow up, but we'll see!

My name is *Ashley Cofell*. I live in a small town in Minnesota. I'm 10 years old. I started writing books when I was seven or eight. I have written four books, which I have given to friends and family. I like to read short stories, especially scary ones. I also like to play soccer, swim, cook, ride my bike, go to the theater, and sing. I've been in two choirs. I want to be a writer and a doctor when I grow up.

My name is *Morgan Fykes*. I'm 12 years old, and I live in a large old house with a big porch and a room of my own in Washington, D.C. I'm in sixth grade at a private school for girls. I'm cheerful and I talk a lot, except when I'm meeting new people. My mom and I started a mother-daughter book club three years ago, and we wrote a book about the club. It was published last year, and I went on a book tour and did presentations on my own. I have an art section set up in one corner of my basement, and I also like dancing (tap, ballet, and jazz), sports, and camping.

My name is *Katie Hedberg*. I have a younger sister named Mollie and a younger brother named Sam. I also have an older half-brother named Daniel. I'm 11 years old and in sixth grade in Minnesota. I like to go shopping, hang with my friends, listen to CDs, read magazines, and do stuff that a normal 11-year-old would do. I play the piano and the trumpet and sing in choir. I had a chapter in the book *Girls Know Best*. I'm a Girl Scout and I help with my younger sister's troop.

My name is **Elizabeth Larsson** and I live near Philadelphia. Among many things, one of my passions is dancing. I love to dance, especially ballet. When I grow up, I probably want to go into the profession of sports medicine for dancers, or physical therapy. Other things I like to do are read, write, play on the computer, and anything that involves making something. I have my own business making silk eye pillows, filled with little seeds, to help you relax. My favorite foods are pizza, baked ziti, and chocolate. I go to an all-girls school, and I'm Quaker. I'm in the seventh grade.

I'm **Priscilla Mendoza**. I like listening to music, being outdoors, traveling, and trying new things. Soccer, gymnastics, and basketball are some of my favorite sports. My favorite color is lavender. On rainy days I like to grab a couple of friends and veg out on the couch to a couple of comedy or horror flicks. I'm 11 and in the seventh grade. I live in a college town in northern California. Someday I hope to be a journalist, a lawyer, or the president of my very own company...who knows? (But for now I'll stick to baby-sitting.)

Julia Peters-Axtell is from a small city in Minnesota. I used to be on the *New Moon* magazine board but decided to try something new, like this! I'm in eighth grade at a public high school. I have a little sister — Emma — and my two parents, who I love to death. My favorite things are: my parents, guys, my sister, gum, my friends, my cats, music, cappuccino, and dances. I love all kinds of sports, but especially I enjoy soccer, track, and softball. I am on the JV soccer and track teams.

My name is **Caitlin Stern** and I live in a small town in Alaska. I un-school, which means that I choose what I learn and how I learn it. I've played the piano since I was five (I'm 13 now), and the recorder since I was eight. I'm also learning Japanese. I like jogging, biking, ice skating, and downhill skiing. I like to read books by Philip Pullman, Jules Verne, and Daniel Quinn. I listen to rock mostly, especially the Beatles and Sean Lennon. I'm a Libra. I love hanging out with my friends, but most of them don't live in Alaska. I have lived in a lot of different places, like New Zealand, Bali, Hawaii, and England.

THE NEW MOON BOOKS GIRLS EDITORIAL BOARD

BACK ROW, LEFT TO RIGHT: Julia Peters-Axtell, Katie Hedberg, Flynn Berry, Morgan Fykes, Lauren Calhoun, Caitlin Stern, Priscilla Mendoza

FRONT ROW: Elizabeth Larsson, Ashley Cofell

The first convening of the New Moon Books Girls Editorial Board
New York City
May 1998

Celebrate and empower girls and women with New Moon Publishing!

"New Moon Publishing has an agenda for girls and young women that's refreshingly different from mainstream corporate media. New Moon is building a community of girls and young women intent on saving their true selves. New Moon's magazines are a godsend for girls and young women, for their parents and the adults who care about them."

—**Mary Pipher, Ph.D.,** author of *Reviving Ophelia: Saving the Selves of Adolescent Girls*

New Moon: The Magazine for Girls and Their Dreams
Edited by girls ages 8–14, *New Moon* is an ad-free international bimonthly magazine that is a joy to read at any age!

New Moon Network: For Adults Who Care About Girls
Share the successes and strategies of a worldwide network of parents, teachers, and other adults committed to raising healthy, confident girls.

Between the Moon and You
A catalog of delightful gifts that celebrate and educate girls and women. Visit at www.newmooncatalog.com.

New Moon Education Division
A variety of interactive workshops and compelling speakers for conferences or conventions.

For information on any of these New Moon resources, contact:

New Moon Publishing
P.O. Box 3620
Duluth, MN 55803-3620
Toll-free: 800-381-4743 • Fax: 218-728-0314
E-mail: newmoon@newmoon.org
Web site: www.newmoon.org